Key Facts™ on

Hong Kong

~Essential Information on Hong Kong~

By Patrick W. Nee

The Internationalist®

www.internationalist.com

The Internationalist®

International Business, Investment, and Travel

Published by:

The Internationalist Publishing Company

96 Walter Street/ Suite 200

Boston, MA 02131, USA

Tel: 617-354-7722

www.internationalist.com

PN@internationalist.com

Copyright © 2013 by PWN

The Internationalist is a Registered Trademark. "Key Facts" and "The Internationalist Business Guides" are Trademarks of The Internationalist Publishing Company.

All Rights are reserved under International, Pan-American, and Pan-Asian Conventions. No part of this book may be reproduced in any form without the written permission of the publisher. All rights vigorously enforced

Table Of Contents

Chapter 1: Background

Chapter 2: Geography

Chapter 3: People and Society

Chapter 4: Government

Chapter 5: Economy

Chapter 6: Energy

Chapter 7: Communications

Chapter 8: Transportation

Chapter 9: Military

Chapter 10: Transnational Issues

Map of Hong Kong

Chapter 1: Background

Occupied by the UK in 1841, Hong Kong was formally ceded by China the following year; various adjacent lands were added later in the 19th century. Pursuant to an agreement signed by China and the UK on 19 December 1984, Hong Kong became the Hong Kong Special Administrative Region (SAR) of the People's Republic of China on 1 July 1997. In this agreement, China promised that, under its "one country, two systems" formula, China's socialist economic system would not be imposed on Hong Kong and that Hong Kong would enjoy a high degree of autonomy in all matters except foreign and defense affairs for the next 50 years.

Chapter 2: Geography

Location:
    Eastern Asia, bordering the South China Sea and China

Geographic coordinates:
    22 15 N, 114 10 E

Map references:
    Southeast Asia

Area:
    total: 1,104 sq km
    country comparison to the world: 184
    land: 1,054 sq km
    water: 50 sq km

Area - comparative:
    six times the size of Washington, DC

Land boundaries:
    total: 30 km
    regional border: China 30 km

Coastline:
    733 km

Maritime claims:
    territorial sea: 3 nm

Climate:

subtropical monsoon; cool and humid in winter, hot and rainy from spring through summer, warm and sunny in fall

Terrain:

hilly to mountainous with steep slopes; lowlands in north

Elevation extremes:

lowest point: South China Sea 0 m

highest point: Tai Mo Shan 958 m

Natural resources:

outstanding deepwater harbor, feldspar

Land use:

arable land: 5.05%

permanent crops: 1.01%

other: 93.94% (2011)

Irrigated land:

NA; note - included in the total for China

Natural hazards:

occasional typhoons

Environment - current issues:

air and water pollution from rapid urbanization

Environment - international agreements:

party to: Marine Dumping (associate member), Ship Pollution (associate member)

Geography - note:
   composed of more than 200 islands

Chapter 3: People and Society

Nationality:

noun: Chinese/Hong Konger

adjective: Chinese/Hong Kong

Ethnic groups:

Chinese 93.6%, Filipino 1.9%, Indonesian 1.9%, other 2.6% (2011 census)

Languages:

Cantonese (official) 89.5%, English (official) 3.5%, Putonghua (Mandarin) 1.4%, other Chinese dialects 4%, other 1.6% (2011 census)

Religions:

eclectic mixture of local religions 90%, Christian 10%

Population:

7,182,724 (July 2013 est.)

country comparison to the world: 99

Age structure:

0-14 years: 11.3% (male 425,289/female 389,622)

15-24 years: 10.7% (male 398,475/female 372,250)

25-54 years: 48.4% (male 1,627,699/female 1,848,730)

55-64 years: 15.1% (male 538,854/female 547,690)

65 years and over: 14.4% (male 486,043/female 548,072) (2013 est.)

Median age:

total: 44.5 years

male: 43.8 years

female: 45 years (2013 est.)

Population growth rate:

0.39% (2013 est.)

country comparison to the world: 156

Birth rate:

7.58 births/1,000 population (2013 est.)

country comparison to the world: 222

Death rate:

7.39 deaths/1,000 population (2013 est.)

country comparison to the world: 116

Net migration rate:

3.75 migrant(s)/1,000 population (2013 est.)

country comparison to the world: 27

Urbanization:

urban population: 100% of total population (2010)

rate of urbanization: 0.9% annual rate of change (2010-15 est.)

Sex ratio:

at birth: 1.07 male(s)/female

0-14 years: 1.09 male(s)/female
15-24 years: 1.07 male(s)/female
25-54 years: 0.88 male(s)/female
55-64 years: 1 male(s)/female
65 years and over: 0.88 male(s)/female
total population: 0.94 male(s)/female (2013 est.)

Infant mortality rate:

total: 2.89 deaths/1,000 live births

country comparison to the world: 219

male: 3.06 deaths/1,000 live births

female: 2.7 deaths/1,000 live births (2013 est.)

Life expectancy at birth:

total population: 82.2 years

country comparison to the world: 9

male: 79.47 years

female: 85.14 years (2013 est.)

Total fertility rate:

1.11 children born/woman (2013 est.)

country comparison to the world: 221

HIV/AIDS - adult prevalence rate:

0.1% (2003 est.)

country comparison to the world: 128

HIV/AIDS - people living with HIV/AIDS:

2,600 (2003 est.)

country comparison to the world: 131

HIV/AIDS - deaths:
fewer than 200 (2003 est.)

country comparison to the world: 106

Education expenditures:
3.4% of GDP (2011)

country comparison to the world: 129

Literacy:
definition: age 15 and over has ever attended school

total population: 93.5%

male: 96.9%

female: 89.6% (2002)

School life expectancy (primary to tertiary education):
total: 16 years

male: 15 years

female: 16 years (2009)

Unemployment, youth ages 15-24:
total: 9.4%

country comparison to the world: 110

male: 11%

female: 7.9% (2011)

Chapter 4: Government

Country name:

 conventional long form: Hong Kong Special Administrative Region

 conventional short form: Hong Kong

 official long form: Xianggang Tebie Xingzhengqu

 official short form: Xianggang

 abbreviation: HK

Dependency status:

 special administrative region of China

Government type:

 limited democracy

Administrative divisions:

 none (special administrative region of China)

Independence:

 none (special administrative region of China)

National holiday:

 National Day (Anniversary of the Founding of the People's Republic of China), 1 October (1949); note - 1 July 1997 is celebrated as Hong Kong Special Administrative Region Establishment Day

Constitution:

The Basic Law, approved March 1990 by China's National People's Congress, is Hong Kong's charter

Legal system:

mixed legal system of common law based on the English model and Chinese customary law (in matters of family and land tenure)

Suffrage:

18 years of age in direct elections for half the legislature and a majority of seats in 18 district councils; universal for permanent residents living in the territory of Hong Kong for the past seven years; note - in indirect elections, suffrage is limited to about 220,000 members of functional constituencies for the other half of the legislature and an 1,200-member election committee for the chief executive drawn from broad sectoral groupings, central government bodies, municipal organizations, and elected Hong Kong officials

Executive branch:

chief of state: President of China HU Jintao (since 15 March 2003)

head of government: Chief Executive LEUNG Chun-ying [C.Y.LEUNG] (since 1 July 2012) cabinet: Executive Council or ExCo consists of 15 official members and 16 non-official members

elections: chief executive elected for five-year term by a 1,200-member election committee; on 25 March 2012 LEUNG Chun-ying [C.Y.LEUNG] was elected chief executive by a 1,193-member election committee; he took office on 1 July 2012; (next to be held in March 2017)

note: the Legislative Council voted in June 2010 to expand the electoral committee to 1,200 seats for the 2012 selection

election results: LEUNG Chun-ying was selected with 689 votes; Henry TANG received 285 votes, and Albert HO received 76 of the 1,132 votes cast; 82 ballots were deemed invalid; most were blank

Legislative branch:

unicameral Legislative Council or LegCo (70 seats; 35 members indirectly elected by functional constituencies, 35 elected by popular vote; members serve four-year terms)

note: the LegCo voted in June 2010 to expand to 70 seats for the 2012 election; the measure was approved by the National People's Congress Standing Committee in August 2010 elections: last held on 9 September 2012 (next to be held in September 2016)

election results: percent of vote by block - pro-democracy 56%; pro-Beijing 41%, independent 3%; seats by parties - (pro-Beijing 43) DAB 13, BRA 7, FTU 6, Liberal Party 5, others 10; (pro-democracy 27) Democratic Party 6, Civic Party 6, Labor Party 4, People Power 3, Professional Commons 3, League of Social Democrats 1, ADPL 1, PTU 1, Neo Democrats 1, NWSC 1; independent 1

Judicial branch:

Court of Final Appeal, High Court (Court of Appeal and the Court of the First Instance), district courts, magistrates' courts, and other special courts

Political parties and leaders:

parties: Association for Democracy and People's Livelihood or ADPL [LIU Sung Lee]; Business and Professional Alliance [Andrew LEUNG]; Civic Party [EU Audrey]; Democratic Alliance for the Betterment and Progress of Hong Kong or DAB [TAM Yiu-cheng]; Democratic Party [Emily LAU]; Labor Party [LEE Cheuk-yan]; League of Social Democrats or LSD [LEUNG Kwok-hung]; Liberal Party [Selina CHOW]; Neo Democrats [joint leaders]; New

People's Party [Regina IP Lau Su-yee]; People Power [Raymond WONG Yuk-man]

<u>others</u>: Confederation of Trade Unions or CTU; Federation of Trade Unions or FTU; Neighborhood and Workers Service Center or NWSC; Professional Commons (think tank) [Charles MOK]; Professional Teachers Union or PTU

<u>note</u>: political blocs include: pro-democracy - ADPL, Civic Party, Democratic Party, Labor Party, League of Social Democrats, People Power, Professional Commons; pro-Beijing - DAB, FTU, Liberal Party, New People's Party, The Business and Professional Alliance; there is no political party ordinance, so there are no registered political parties; politically active groups register as societies or companies

Political pressure groups and leaders:

Chinese General Chamber of Commerce (pro-China); Chinese Manufacturers' Association of Hong Kong; Confederation of Trade Unions or CTU (pro-democracy) [LEE Cheuk-yan, general secretary]; Federation of Hong Kong Industries; Federation of Trade Unions or FTU (pro-China) [CHENG Yiu-tong, executive councilor]; Hong Kong Alliance in Support of the Patriotic Democratic Movement in

China [LEE Cheuk-yan, chairman]; Hong Kong and Kowloon Trade Union Council (pro-Taiwan); Hong Kong General Chamber of Commerce; Hong Kong Professional Teachers' Union [FUNG Wai-wah, president]; Neighborhood and Workers' Service Center or NWSC [LEUNG Yiu-chung, LegCo member] (pro-democracy); Civic Act-up [Cyd HO Sau-lan, LegCo member] (pro-democracy)

International organization participation:
ADB, APEC, BIS, FATF, ICC (national committees), IHO, IMF, IMO (associate), Interpol (subbureau), IOC, ISO (correspondent), ITUC (NGOs), UNWTO (associate), UPU, WCO, WTO

Diplomatic representation in the US:
none (special administrative region of China); Hong Kong Economic and Trade Office (HKETO) carries out normal liaison and communication with the US Government and other US entities
representative: Donald TONG
office: 1520 18th Street NW, Washington, DC 20036
telephone: [1] 202 331-8947
FAX: [1] 202 331-8958
HKETO offices: New York, San Francisco

Diplomatic representation from the US:

chief of mission: Consul General Stephen M. YOUNG

consulate(s) general: 26 Garden Road, Hong Kong

mailing address: Unit 8000, Box 1, DPO AP 96521-0006

telephone: [852] 2523-9011

FAX: [852] 2845-1598

Flag description:

red with a stylized, white, five-petal Bauhinia flower in the center; each petal contains a small, red, five-pointed star in its middle; the red color is the same as that on the Chinese flag and represents the motherland; the fragrant Bauhinia - developed in Hong Kong the late 19th century - has come to symbolize the region; the five stars echo those on the flag of China

National symbol(s):

orchid tree flower

National anthem:

note: as a Special Administrative Region of China, "Yiyonggjun Jinxingqu" is the official anthem

Chapter 5: Economy

Economy - overview:

Hong Kong has a free market economy, highly dependent on international trade and finance - the value of goods and services trade, including the sizable share of re-exports, is about four times GDP. Hong Kong levies excise duties on only four commodities, namely: hard alcohol, tobacco, hydrocarbon oil, and methyl alcohol. There are no quotas or dumping laws. Hong Kong's open economy left it exposed to the global economic slowdown that began in 2008. Although increasing integration with China, through trade, tourism, and financial links, helped it to make an initial recovery more quickly than many observers anticipated, it again faces a possible slowdown as exports to the Euro zone and US slump. The Hong Kong government is promoting the Special Administrative Region (SAR) as the site for Chinese renminbi (RMB) internationalization. Hong Kong residents are allowed to establish RMB-denominated savings accounts; RMB-denominated corporate and Chinese government bonds have been issued in Hong Kong; and RMB trade settlement is allowed. The territory far exceeded the RMB conversion quota set by Beijing for trade settlements in 2010 due to the growth of earnings from exports to the mainland. RMB deposits grew to roughly 9.1% of total system deposits in Hong Kong by the end of 2012, an increase of 59% from the previous year. The government is pursuing efforts to introduce additional use of RMB in Hong Kong financial markets and is seeking to expand the RMB quota. The mainland has long been Hong Kong's largest trading partner, accounting for about half of Hong Kong's exports by value. Hong Kong's natural resources are limited, and food and raw materials must be imported. As a result of China's easing of travel restrictions, the number of mainland tourists to the territory has surged from 4.5 million in 2001 to 34.9 million in 2012, outnumbering visitors from all other countries combined. Hong Kong has also established itself as the premier stock market for Chinese firms seeking to list abroad. In 2012 mainland Chinese companies constituted about 46.6% of the firms listed on the Hong Kong Stock Exchange and accounted for about 57.4% of the Exchange's market capitalization. During the past decade, as Hong Kong's manufacturing industry moved to the mainland, its service industry has grown rapidly. Growth slowed to 5% in 2011, and less than 2% in 2012. Credit expansion and tight housing supply conditions caused Hong Kong property prices to rise rapidly and inflation to rise 4.1% in 2012. Lower and middle income segments of the population are increasingly unable to afford adequate housing. Hong Kong continues to link its currency closely to the US dollar, maintaining an arrangement established in 1983.

GDP (purchasing power parity):
$363.7 billion (2012 est.)
country comparison to the world: 36
$357.2 billion (2011 est.)
$340.1 billion (2010 est.)
note: data are in 2012 US dollars

GDP (official exchange rate):
$261.6 billion (2012 est.)

GDP - real growth rate:
1.8% (2012 est.)
country comparison to the world: 144
5% (2011 est.)
7.1% (2010 est.)

GDP - per capita (PPP):

$50,700 (2012 est.)

country comparison to the world: 13

$50,200 (2011 est.)

$48,200 (2010 est.)

note: data are in 2012 US dollars

GDP - composition by sector:

agriculture: 0%

industry: 7%

services: 93% (2012 est.)

Labor force:

3.826 million (2012 est.)

country comparison to the world: 94

Labor force - by occupation:

manufacturing: 4%

construction: 2.7%

wholesale and retail trade, restaurants, and hotels: 40.9%

financing, insurance, and real estate: 12.5%

transport and communications: 9.9%

community and social services: 16.9%

note: above data exclude public sector (2012 est.)

Unemployment rate:

3.3% (2012 est.)

country comparison to the world: 28

3.4% (2011 est.)

Population below poverty line:

NA%

Household income or consumption by percentage share:

lowest 10%: NA%

highest 10%: NA%

Distribution of family income - Gini index:

53.7 (2011)

country comparison to the world: 11

53.3 (2007)

Investment (gross fixed):

26.3% of GDP (2012 est.)

country comparison to the world: 42

Budget:

revenues: $57.12 billion

expenditures: $48.79 billion (2012 est.)

Taxes and other revenues:

21.8% of GDP (2012 est.)

country comparison to the world: 144

Budget surplus (+) or deficit (-):

3.2% of GDP (2012 est.)

country comparison to the world: 17

Public debt:

30% of GDP (2012 est.)

country comparison to the world: 114

39.8% of GDP (2011 est.)

Inflation rate (consumer prices):

4.1% (2012 est.)

country comparison to the world: 118

5.3% (2011 est.)

Central bank discount rate:

0.5% (31 December 2012)

country comparison to the world: 135

0.5% (31 December 2011)

Commercial bank prime lending rate:

5% (31 December 2012 est.)

country comparison to the world: 158

5% (31 December 2011 est.)

Stock of narrow money:

$176.6 billion (31 December 2012 est.)

country comparison to the world: 21

$144.5 billion (31 December 2011 est.)

Stock of broad money:

$1.148 trillion (31 December 2012 est.)

country comparison to the world: 16

$1.033 trillion (31 December 2011 est.)

Stock of domestic credit:

$714 billion (31 December 2012 est.)

country comparison to the world: 21

$651.4 billion (31 December 2011 est.)

Market value of publicly traded shares:

$2.81 trillion (31 December 2012)

country comparison to the world: 6

$2.24 trillion (31 December 2011)

$2.711 trillion (31 December 2010 est.)

Agriculture - products:

fresh vegetables; poultry, pork; fish

Industries:

textiles, clothing, tourism, banking, shipping, electronics, plastics, toys, watches, clocks

Industrial production growth rate:

-0.1% (2012 est.)

country comparison to the world: 147

Current account balance:

$6.4 billion (2012 est.)

country comparison to the world: 28

$14.1 billion (2011 est.)

Exports:

$439 billion (2012 est.)

country comparison to the world: 13

$438 billion (2011 est.)

Exports - commodities:

electrical machinery and appliances, textiles, apparel, footwear, watches and clocks, toys, plastics, precious stones, printed material

Exports - partners:
China 54.1%, US 9.9%, Japan 4% (2012 est.)

Imports:
$499.4 billion (2012 est.)

country comparison to the world: 10

$494.1 billion (2011 est.)

Imports - commodities:
raw materials and semi-manufactures, consumer goods, capital goods, foodstuffs, fuel (most is reexported)

Imports - partners:
China 46.9%, Japan 8.4%, Taiwan 7.5%, South Korea 5%, US 4.7% (2012 est.)

Reserves of foreign exchange and gold:
$317.3 billion (31 December 2012 est.)

country comparison to the world: 10

$285.4 billion (31 December 2011 est.)

Debt - external:
$995.4 billion (30 September 2012 est.)

country comparison to the world: 17

$903.2 billion (30 June 2011 est.)

Stock of direct foreign investment - at home:
$1.2 trillion (31 December 2012 est.)
country comparison to the world: 4
$1.138 trillion (31 December 2011 est.)

Stock of direct foreign investment - abroad:
$1.112 trillion (31 December 2012 est.)
country comparison to the world: 5
$1.046 trillion (31 December 2011 est.)

Exchange rates:
Hong Kong dollars (HKD) per US dollar -
7.76 (2012 est.)
7.78 (2011 est.)
7.77 (2010 est.)
7.75 (2009)
7.75 (2008)

Fiscal year:
1 April - 31 March

Chapter 6: Energy

Electricity - production:
41.3 billion kWh (2012 est.)
country comparison to the world: 57

Electricity - consumption:
45.07 billion kWh (2012 est.)
country comparison to the world: 50

Electricity - exports:
497.4 million kWh (2012 est.)
country comparison to the world: 61

Electricity - imports:
11.15 billion kWh (2012 est.)
country comparison to the world: 18

Electricity - installed generating capacity:
10.66 million kW (2012 est.)
country comparison to the world: 53

Electricity - from fossil fuels:
100% of total installed capacity (2012 est.)
country comparison to the world: 18

Electricity - from nuclear fuels:
0% of total installed capacity (2012 est.)
country comparison to the world: 105

Electricity - from hydroelectric plants:

0% of total installed capacity (2012 est.)

country comparison to the world: 176

Electricity - from other renewable sources:

0% of total installed capacity (2012 est.)

country comparison to the world: 139

Crude oil - production:

0 bbl/day (2012 est.)

country comparison to the world: 146

Crude oil - exports:

0 bbl/day (2012 est.)

country comparison to the world: 124

Crude oil - imports:

0 bbl/day (2012 est.)

country comparison to the world: 198

Crude oil - proved reserves:

0 bbl (1 January 2012 es)

country comparison to the world: 145

Refined petroleum products - production:

0 bbl/day (2012 est.)

country comparison to the world: 158

Refined petroleum products - consumption:

337,600 bbl/day (2012 est.)

country comparison to the world: 38

Refined petroleum products - exports:

16,520 bbl/day (2012)

country comparison to the world: 78

Refined petroleum products - imports:

354,100 bbl/day (2012 est.)

country comparison to the world: 19

Natural gas - production:

0 cu m (2012 est.)

country comparison to the world: 143

Natural gas - consumption:

2.79 billion cu m (2012 est.)

country comparison to the world: 76

Natural gas - exports:

0 cu m (2012 est.)

country comparison to the world: 115

Natural gas - imports:

2.79 billion cu m (2012 est.)

country comparison to the world: 45

Natural gas - proved reserves:

0 cu m (1 January 2012 es)

country comparison to the world: 148

Carbon dioxide emissions from consumption of energy:

39.3 million Mt (2009 est.)

country comparison to the world: 71

Chapter 7: Communications

Telephones - main lines in use:
>4.342 million (2011)
>country comparison to the world: 38

Telephones - mobile cellular:
>15.293 million (2011)
>country comparison to the world: 55

Telephone system:
>general assessment: modern facilities provide excellent domestic and international services
>
>domestic: microwave radio relay links and extensive fiber-optic network
>
>international: country code - 852; multiple international submarine cables provide connections to Asia, US, Australia, the Middle East, and Western Europe; satellite earth stations - 3 Intelsat (1 Pacific Ocean and 2 Indian Ocean); coaxial cable to Guangzhou, China (2012)

Broadcast media:
>2 commercial terrestrial TV networks each with multiple stations; multi-channel satellite and cable TV systems available; 3 radio networks, one of which is

government-funded, operate about 15 radio stations (2012)

Internet country code:

.hk

Internet hosts:

870,041 (2012)

country comparison to the world: 48

Internet users:

4.873 million (2009)

country comparison to the world: 47

Chapter 8: Transportation

Airports:

    2 (2012)

    country comparison to the world: 201

Airports - with paved runways:

    total: 2

    over 3,047 m: 1

    1,524 to 2,437 m: 1 (2012)

Heliports:

    9 (2012)

Roadways:

    total: 2,067 km

    country comparison to the world: 172

    paved: 2,067 km (2010)

Merchant marine:

    total: 1,644

    country comparison to the world: 5

    by type: barge carrier 2, bulk carrier 785, cargo 198, carrier 10, chemical tanker 149, container 288, liquefied gas 31, passenger 4, passenger/cargo 9, petroleum tanker 156, roll on/roll off 5, vehicle carrier 7 foreign-owned: 976 (Bangladesh 1, Belgium 26, Bermuda 20, Canada 77, China 500, Cyprus 3, Denmark 42, France 4, Germany 10, Greece 27, Indonesia 10, Iran 3, Japan 79, Libya 1, Norway 48, Russia 1, Singapore 13, South Korea 3, Switzerland 5, Taiwan 25, UAE 1, UK 33, US 44)

registered in other countries: 341 (Bahamas 3, Bermuda 4, Cambodia 10, China 18, Curacao 1, Cyprus 2, Georgia 3, India 2, Kiribati 2, Liberia 48, Malaysia 8, Malta 4, Marshall Islands 3, NZ 1, Panama 144, Saint Vincent and the Grenadines 5, Seychelles 1, Sierra Leone 7, Singapore 46, Thailand 1, UK 12, unknown 16) (2010)

Ports and terminals:

Hong Kong

Chapter 9: Military

Military branches:
> no regular indigenous military forces; Hong Kong garrison of China's People's Liberation Army (PLA) includes elements of the PLA Ground Forces, PLA Navy, and PLA Air Force; these forces are under the direct leadership of the Central Military Commission in Beijing and under administrative control of the adjacent Guangzhou Military Region (2012)

Manpower available for military service:
> males age 16-49: 1,704,090
> females age 16-49: 1,873,175 (2010 est.)

Manpower fit for military service:
> males age 16-49: 1,387,213
> females age 16-49: 1,505,875 (2010 est.)

Manpower reaching militarily significant age annually:
> male: 39,579
> female: 36,554 (2010 est.)

Military expenditures:
> NA

Military - note:
> defense is the responsibility of China

Chapter 10: Transnational Issues

Disputes - international:
   none

Illicit drugs:
   despite strenuous law enforcement efforts, faces difficult challenges in controlling transit of heroin and methamphetamine to regional and world markets; modern banking system provides conduit for money laundering; rising indigenous use of synthetic drugs, especially among young people

Map of Hong Kong

Other Key Facts™ Titles

Key Facts on Syria

Key Facts on China

Key Facts on Qatar

Key Facts on India

Key Facts on Germany

Key Facts on Argentina

Key Facts on Russia

Key Facts on North Korea

Key Facts on Brazil

Key Facts on Italy

Key Facts on the United Arab Emirates

Key Facts on the European Union

Key Facts on Pakistan

Key Facts on Saudi Arabia

Key Facts on Cyprus

Key Facts on Iran

Key Facts on Afghanistan

Key Facts on Iraq

Key Facts on Indonesia

Key Facts on South Korea

Key Facts on France

Key Facts on the United Kingdom

Key Facts on Egypt

Key Facts on Israel

Key Facts on Mexico

Key Facts on the United States of America

Key Facts on Turkey

Key Facts on South Africa

Key Facts on Greece

Key Facts on Japan

Key Facts on Malaysia

Key Facts on Vietnam

All Key Facts™ Titles are Available at

www.Amazon.com

THE INTERNATIONALIST®

2013

WWW.INTERNATIONALIST.COM

www.ingramcontent.com/pod-product-compliance
Lightning Source LLC
Chambersburg PA
CBHW071549170526
45166CB00004B/1599